MW00942649

ELLA'S GOLDEN EGGS

ELLA'S GOLDEN EGGS

HOW TO CONQUER REAL ESTATE
AND NEVER BE BROKE AGAIN

Ella M. Coney

Copyright © 2016 **Ella M. Coney**
All rights reserved.

ISBN-13: **9781532719707**
ISBN-10: **1532719701**
Library of Congress Control Number: **2016906509**
CreateSpace Independent Publishing Platform
North Charleston, South Carolina

CONTENTS

DISCLAIMER

The names and other identifying information about many of the characters in this book have been changed to protect their privacy.

This book is dedicated to my mama, Josie Cooper. At 86 years old she is in the final stages of her life. She has accomplished so much. This book is also dedicated to my sisters, who are doing everything possible to make sure our mama spends her last days in the serenity of her own home. Mama scrimped, scraped, and struggled to provide us a home so we would know stability. Now this same home will provide her peace and comfort in her last days.
We love you, Mama!

INTRODUCTION

I hear them whispering, "Really, *she* is a millionaire?"

"Well, yeah," is the reply. I just smile and go on.

I am not trying to wear my money on my back. I want to make sure it is in my pocketbook. If you have ever visited the land of the flat broke and made it out, you know that is not a place you ever want to visit again. My money now gives me options in life that were not previously available to me.

It gives me some semblance of control over the destiny of my life and the lives of my children and family members.

My first book was entitled, *When You Fall Down-Get Up!* If you get a chance, please pick up a copy. It tells the story about how I started out on welfare, living in the housing projects, and ended up becoming a real estate millionaire. It is a good read, full of sex, violence, drama and all the things you go through in life when you are young and trying to find your way.

Everyone commented that I had made a million dollars, but I did not share the details of how I accomplished this feat. I will share many of the details of this transformation in this book, along with my thought patterns throughout my journey. You will share my triumphs and my disasters. You will learn how you, too, can make the journey. It is this women's key to never being broke again.

I told many people that after they read my story, they would ask themselves, "Do I really want to go through what she went through to get to where she got to?"

It was a roller-coaster ride full of ups and downs. My pastor always told us, if we were "faithful over the seed we would be rewarded with the harvest." The reward was beyond anything I could have ever imagined. I did it because that was my dream. I did it for my children. It is what kept me going. I always believed I could. I was going to be a real estate millionaire.

You are not going to believe what I am telling you. You are certainly not going to do it. It is much easier to have fun now and think about it later. But I am telling you, if you are a good steward over your money now, there is peace of mind and prosperity down the road, greater than anything you can imagine.

Keep your eye on the prize through all of the following:

- marriage
- childbirth
- sickness
- divorce

- death
- devastation

You have to keep going when you do not know where you will get the strength. Ask a higher power. Ask the universe. Put it out there. In the end the one who wins is the one who thinks he or she can!

It can be done. It won't happen overnight. It is a steady, continuous process over time. You can get there. If I could do it, anyone can do it. I am not firing on all cylinders, but I know what I want.

As you read my story, you might say, "It took a long time to accumulate those assets. I will be old if I follow that plan." Life is short. You are going to get old anyway. You can be old and broke or old with money trees and golden eggs.

Take the first step on the journey to your financial freedom. There are no shortcuts to anywhere worth going. You can get there.

CHAPTER 1

WHERE DO YOU WANT TO GO?

It is important to have concrete financial goals in life. You have to know where you want to go financially. You also have to have a tangible plan that lays out how you are going to get there. My goal of being a real estate millionaire was firmly planted in my head.

My adult life started early. I was pregnant at seventeen years old. Before I got past my eighteenth birthday, I had two children. Circumstances forced me to grow up quickly.

With the first baby, Mama allowed me to stay in the warm, secure, and loving family home she had created for us. After the second baby, Mama let me know she could not take care of me and all my babies. She was still raising her own children. If I insisted on continuing to have all these babies, I needed to get out on my own and figure things out for myself. I was forced to make some really tough decisions.

A downtown department store gave me a job as a salesperson. People said I carried myself well.

It was hard staying on my feet for eight hours a day. I had never really worked before. But if my mama could work as a hotel maid—scrubbing other people's toilets and floors and making their beds—I could work just as hard. She said it took money to pay the bills. You need a job to get money, and you do whatever that job wants you to do. You need that job to take care of your family. If scrubbing toilets and floors was not beneath her, surely I could walk around for eight hours a day looking pretty, while helping other women choose things that helped them look pretty.

The neighbor girl across the street and I got a little two-bedroom apartment. We were both working, and we split the rent and utilities in half. I shared my room with my two young children.

That arrangement only lasted a few months. My roommate lost her job and moved in with her boyfriend. I could not pay all the rent on my own, and the landlord was nice enough to break the lease. In exchange for his kindness, I left the apartment immaculate. All he had to do was move someone else in.

In my desperation to put a stable roof over the heads of my two children and me, I moved into the Westwood Housing Projects. My rent was three dollars per month.

The projects were a hellhole. There were giant rats and roaches. If my kids dared to venture outside the front door, they saw unspeakable crimes and violence. Young girls were gang raped, and young boys suffered brutal gang beatings. Drug deals, fires, vandalism, and anything else you could imagine happened all the time.

This environment depressed my soul. In these difficult times, I met a good friend named Mae Coleman. Each time we visited, we would talk and dream about the day we got out of the projects. We each were going to buy our own houses and have nice cars that did not break down when you drove them around the corner. We were going to have great careers that paid enough so that we would have extra money in the bank. We would be able to eat out periodically at nice restaurants and take a real vacation every once in a while.

We did not want to be crazy rich. We just wanted to get out of the Westwood Housing Projects. All we had to hold on to were our dreams.

I was young and had never been on welfare before. I do not know where I got the notion that you did not have to report employment unless it lasted longer than thirty days. It does not matter. I did not report my income, and I was in big trouble. My benefits were terminated, and I was looking at jail time.

My three-dollar rent was three months past due. No more money was coming from the welfare department. My last dead-end job had ended, and I had no source of income. With no money, no job, overdue rent, and a possible jail sentence, the future looked dark.

I told my friend Mae that I was going into the military. It paid $600 a month, provided medical and dental benefits, and offered thirty days a year paid vacation. If I worked for twenty years, I could retire and collect a retirement pension for the rest of my life. This all sounded good to me. It was the answer to my prayers.

I begged Mae to come with me. She thought about it and declined. It just did not seem like the right path for her. We hugged each other tightly, and she wished me well. Time was not my friend. I had to act quickly. I knew where I wanted to go; I just had no idea what it would take to get there.

I could see the light of opportunity getting smaller and smaller. A voice in the dark said, "I have prepared a way out for you. Take your children and go." I grabbed my two children and ran as fast as I could into the light. We made it just before that window of opportunity closed completely.

Finally, I thought, we can rest now. It is going to be okay. I opened my eyes, and we were in the middle of utter chaos. There were soldiers marching, airplanes flying over, and people yelling and screaming. I had gone out of the frying pan into the fire. "Where are we?" I asked. A voice said, "You are in the Air Force now. You can do it—*go!*"

The next seven years were the hardest of my life. The kids and I were tested over and over. We were blazing a trail that not many had dared to take in the military. Over the years it became obvious why. I was one of the first black female aircraft radar technicians in the Air Force, and I had young children. I was a military test case.

My goal—my dream—was to be the highest-paid, highest-ranking black woman in the US Air

Force. I was going to get that house for the kids and myself. I was going to get that nice car and have money in the bank. Things don't always work out like we plan, though. Finally, I broke into a million pieces. I told myself many times, Maybe I should have just stayed in the projects.

I came home from the military a broken creature. With my tail between my legs, I had to admit to my mama that I now had three children, was sick, had very little money and at almost 30 years old, I had no place for my family to stay.

Mama, again, welcomed us into her warm, comfortable, loving home. She had warned me not to go off to the military with children. She was right again. I had crashed and burned and now needed help. She never said "I told you so." We both put all that behind us and never talked about those deep wounds again.

By deciding to go into the Air Force, however, I was rewarded with a disability pension from the military as a thank-you for my service. It was not big. But it was enough to buy a little house, stock it with food, and keep the heat and lights on. If I handled the money carefully, I could guarantee our security for the rest of our lives.

Being a military veteran also came with some incredible benefits. I would be paid to go to college and become educated; there were also medical benefits. I could buy a house with nothing down. I was given preferential treatment for government job assignments and there were many more benefits. I took advantage of almost every single benefit. These benefits really lifted me to a different level in life.

God was not done with us after my time in the military. I went on to become a real-estate millionaire. How this was done will be revealed later in this book. There is a God that sits high and looks low. He knows all things. Read on to find out how I did it.

Oprah Winfrey once said, "One of my greatest lessons has been that what looks like a dark patch in the quest for success is the universe pointing you in a new direction." There can be an opportunity, a blessing, or a miracle in anything, if you can just see it that way.

My first lesson was that you are going to get knocked down many times by life. That is not the end of the story. When you fall down, get up. Keep getting up! Only when you keep on trying can you really succeed, the way that only you can. I read in a book once that you have to believe that "God sees you in your darkness and your sunlit dawn is near." Keep moving forward one step at a time. Quitting is not an option!!

CHAPTER 2

FINANCIAL GOALS

The military paid $600 a month. That was three times more than I had made as a salesperson and more money than I had ever made in my life. I was twenty years old.

I knew that if I managed the money wisely, it would provide a very good living for me and my kids. My first goal was to get a dependable car. It was extremely difficult getting around with two kids on the bus. In the winter it was inhumane punishment.

My second goal was to save $50,000 before I turned thirty years old. This was a lofty goal, but I really felt I could do it. I remembered the saying, "If you believe it, then you can achieve it." The $50,000 goal was locked in my brain.

Age	Money Saved
20	$500
21	$1,000
22	$1,500
23	$2,000
24	$3,000
25	$4,500
26	$5,500
27	$6,500
28	$7,500
29	$8,500
30	$9,500
Total Saved	$50,000

My final goal was to buy a house for myself and the kids. They needed a backyard that was safe for them to play in and a sidewalk on which to ride their bikes and skateboards. We needed a home of our own.

I was able to accomplish the first goal of buying a car fairly quickly. Michael, my estranged husband, agreed to cosign for me when I bought it. He had good credit. Women could not get anything in the early '70s. The only thing on the lot was a red Toyota stick shift.

Michael did not need to make a down payment; he got financing for three years. The payment was sixty dollars per month. We got the papers signed. I got the key. Now I just had to figure out how to drive a stick shift.

Michael took me to an empty parking lot and gave me a quick lesson. I had to learn to drive with two feet instead of one. Everything only worked if the clutch was engaged. Within thirty minutes, I was driving down the street jerking every time I used the clutch. It was not pretty, but I had my own car.

After a few days, my driving was a lot smoother. One day, though, the car just stopped on me. I could not figure out what was wrong. A nice man came to help me. He looked under the hood and tried to give the battery a boost, but the car would not go. Finally, he asked to get behind the wheel. He looked at all the gauges in the car and noticed that the gas hand was on *E* (empty). The nice man asked me, "When was the last time you put gas in the car?"

I looked puzzled and said, "Gas?" He laughed. He took a red gas can out of his truck and put a little gas in the carburetor and the rest in the tank. My car started right up.

He pointed to the gas station up the street and said, "You need to put gas in your car for it to work." He also showed me how to check the oil and where to fill it up when it was empty. This man was so nice to me, and I was so thankful. God sends angels in your life just when you need them. I learned that you have to take care of your car in order for it to take care of you. This also pertains to your money.

My goal of saving $50,000 by the time I was thirty years old came a little harder. I had a gambling habit. Every time I got $2, I would go to the dog track and bet on a dog. My hope was to win enough to buy a house and put $50,000 in the bank.

I went to the dog track almost every night after work. Hitting "the big one" was just within my reach. I just had to pick the right dog. Each night I went home sad, broke, and disappointed. I did not hit the big one. All my money was gone, and I had nothing to show for it.

One day I said to myself, "This just doesn't make any sense. I will never give the dog track another dime of my money." From then on, when I got $2, I would put it in this big jar in my room. Before I knew it, the jar had grown to $10, and then $20. Within a few months, I was able to take $100 and put it into the bank. By the end of the first year I had $500.

The first budget I ever saw was at sixteen years old. It was on piece of paper and belonged to a lady for whom I babysat. It was a secret weapon in managing your money. You have to know what is coming in and what is going out, or you are shooting in the dark.

The budget was simple.

Income per Month	Dollar Amount
Paycheck on the 1st	$280
Paycheck on the 15th	$280
Total:	**$560**

Expenses per Month	Dollar Amount
House payment	$200
Food	$90
Lights	$40
Water	$15
Babysitter	$100
Carpool	$50
Total:	**$495**

Income per Month ($560) – Expenses per Month ($495) = Saved Money ($65)

A friend of mine told me that when he first got a job, he worked just to get high. All of his money went toward drugs and alcohol. Then a mandatory drug-testing policy was implemented at his job, and he knew that if he wanted to keep his job, he had to give up the drugs and alcohol. It was a good job.

A year later, he noticed he had $15,000 in his bank account. This was money he saved because he was no longer doing drugs and alcohol. He did not realize he was blowing so much of his money until he saw how it added up. He bought a house with the money he saved and equipped it with nice furniture and a tough stereo system. He also bought a new car and still had money left over. It is not how much money you make, but what you do with it. You need to manage your money and not let it manage you.

The goal of owning my own home and saving $50,000 by the time I was thirty years old seemed miles away. I stated my goals out loud. I told my friends and family what my goals were. I wrote them down on two pieces of paper. I put one on the door to my room and looked at it every day as I was leaving for work. I folded the second one and put in my purse. I took it out and looked at it often. I wanted to reach my goal.

One day the house next door to my mama's house went up for sale. The Realtor was doing something over there. I was in my air force uniform and asked if I could see it. The price was $27,000. The Realtor showed it to me and said, "Why don't you buy it?" I told him there was no way I could buy a house. I was a woman. The Realtor started talking really fast about the Equal Credit Opportunity Act. He said it protected the rights of women to buy what they could afford. He told me I was a veteran and did not need to put any money down if I used my military GI Bill. The Realtor said all I needed was good credit and a job. I had both. The payment was only $224 a month. Before I knew what hit me, I was signing a contract on the hood of his car; I was buying this house.

There was only one small catch. I had to put up $200 in earnest money. The Realtor said I would get the money back at closing. It was just to show the owner I had something on the line and was serious about buying the house. I went to the bank, and of course, the $200 was there with money left over. This money was the result of saving my money over the last year instead of giving it away to the dog track. I wrote a check for the Realtor, and I was under contract to buy a house.

I got no sleep for three days. At night I tossed and turned. What was I thinking? How could I buy a house with thirty years of mortgage payments? There must be a way out.

I called the Realtor, and I explained that I had changed my mind and no longer wanted to buy the house. He said, "No problem. We will tear up the contract. You are aware of the fact that you will lose your $200 earnest money deposit."

It took me almost a year to save that money. I could not just walk away from it. After a long silence, I told the Realtor I would go through with the contract.

The whole universe was working on my behalf. I just did not yet realize it. Achieving my goals was closer to my grasp than I realized.

CHAPTER 3

CAN YOU HEAR ME GOD?

I asked God for a bunch of money. I let him know that this would make me happy and would solve all my problems. God does not always give you what you think you want. But he will always give you what you need. Instead of giving me a lot of money, God gave me my own house.

I spoke to God again. "I know you are very busy. You might have me confused with someone else. I asked for money, but I accidentally got a house."

God replied, "This house is how I will bless you." I know that he knows what he is doing, so my kids and I took the house and made it our own.

We cleaned and fixed and planted flowers and grass. But I struggled to pay the $224 house payment, gas, electric, and water bills while still having enough to buy food to eat. Plus, something was always broken. Instead of calling the landlord, I, as the owner, had to get things fixed. I got a second job as a waitress and went to college at night on the military GI Bill. It was hard trying to make enough money to get ahead. And I needed a babysitter. My friend Mae came to my rescue. She had also made it out of the projects and bought a house. Mae ran a child-care service out of her home.

I made the same mistake many young people make. I bought lots of furniture on credit. Of course I had to have a new car in front of my new house. Soon I was in debt way over my head. The bills came faster and faster. I did not realize you have to do things a little bit at a time. Only when you pay for one thing can you then do something else.

We made many sacrifices. I learned to cook the perfect pot of red beans. It took all day, but it was so good. Add a pan of cornbread, and it was the perfect meal. It would last the kids and me four days. The whole pot of beans, with a little meat and the cornbread thrown in, cost less than five dollars. It was a great budget stretcher. We never went hungry.

The struggle taught me to value every cent I had. Money was hard to come by. I could not waste a single penny. I found this was the lesson God needed me to learn. Before he blessed me with a lot of money, I had to first learn the value of a little money.

I discovered four valuable principles in the book *Personal Finance for Dummies,* by Eric Tyson. They served me well. They were as follows:

- Save 10 percent of everything you earn.
- Spend less than you earn.
- Save what you do not spend.
- Invest what you save.

I needed to see the importance of buying things that go up in value.

- Invest in your education. Knowledge can never be taken from you.
- As soon as you can, buy your own home. It will pay you back tenfold.
- Buy stocks and bonds that go up in value. Buy Nike stock instead of ten pairs of Nike shoes.

There is a saying that goes, "If you give a poor mind a million dollars, they will soon lose it. If you take a million dollars from a rich mind, they will soon get it back." My mind had to be prepared. God knew that if he gave me a bunch of money at twenty-two years old, I was going straight to the car dealer to buy a new Mercedes Benz. The next stop would be the department store to get some designer threads. Nothing but the best would do. I would go to the jewelry store and load up on diamonds and gold. This is turning "cash into trash." You pay $60,000 for a car that is only worth $40,000 when you drive it off the lot. It goes down in value $10,000 each year after that. You pay $300 for a pair of shoes, and they lose almost all of their value after you wear them just once.

Only when you have gone after what you want—when you have worked endless hours, gone without, and struggled so hard you did not think you could go on—only then will your prize have value. Only then will you treasure and appreciate that prize. Until then, it will just be one of your endless wants.

When I felt ready, I had to sell the house. I purchased the $27,000 house with $200 in earnest money, paid all the mortgage notes on time, fixed what I could, and in two years walked away after selling the house for $58,000. After paying the home loan in full, I was left with $27,000. That was more money than I had ever seen, and it was mine. I got what I prayed for. The blessing just came to me in a different way than anticipated.

I got my money, but I still did not get a Mercedes Benz. I thought, if one house can make me $27,000 in two years, imagine what three houses can do. It can send me and my now three kids to college. They can then buy a Mercedes Benz for me. An investment now pays never-ending dividends in the future.

Money is not meant to be burned to ashes. It is like a seed. It is meant to be planted so it can grow. I planted seeds that grew into money trees and got my million dollars. I watered, fertilized, pruned, sprayed, and protected these trees. They will sustain me for the rest of my life. If handled properly, they will sustain my children for their lifetimes. These money trees do not provide a lot of money, but I am a simple person. My money trees will pay the mortgage, pay the utilities, buy some food, and provide me with dependable transportation. I will be comfortable for the rest of my life. I know I don't look like a million dollars, but looks are deceiving. Those who look like a million dollars have spent all their money to look that way. It is not how much you make that counts; it is how much you keep.

Many times it was hard getting these money trees to grow. I did without things today so that I would be comfortable tomorrow. I have not been on a vacation in ten years. Once I went on a week-long Caribbean cruise. It cost $3,000, and I had a ball. Quickly, I realized that I could not spend this kind of money every year. It is okay to treat yourself every once in a while, but moderation is the key. Too much partying today puts you in debtor's chains tomorrow. During the times when I was doing well, I planned for what would happen when the party was over. The party did, indeed, end.

I know of countless movie stars and athletes who have made over $50 million a year and who have ended up broke. Their lavish lifestyles are all over the media. They are prime examples of poor money management. Some of these movie stars and athletes have done extremely well however. They are in the minority and are to be emulated. Their example shines brightly as to what can be done.

Over 90 percent of Americans will be blessed with a windfall at some point in their lifetime. Grandma may die, they may hit the lottery, a lawsuit could be settled, or they could land a great job. Will you know what to do when your blessing comes? Will it sustain you for your lifetime, or will your windfall be sucked into a black hole, never to be seen again?

I spent hours every week pouring over figures and projections. I did this by hand, on paper, with a calculator and not a computer program. I am a visual, tactile learner. I have to see, touch, and feel where I am. It has to be real to me. Where am I going? How am I going to get there? What happens if I veer off course? There is a roadblock up ahead. How do I get around it? I fell into a hole. How do I get out of it? A landmine blew up everything. How do I put things back together? I am tired. Why do I have to keep on doing this? How do I stay on track? You sacrifice today for prosperity tomorrow. There is a limit to what a dollar can do, but that dollar is powerful. Make sure it does the best thing for you. The prize is worth the struggle.

An acquaintance of mine called me and said she read my book, *When You Fall Down—Get Up!* She said that they too purchased a home and sold it after four years. They walked away from closing with $61,000. I asked her what she did with the money. She said they took a month-long tour of Europe. They purchased a new car for her husband and a new car for her. They gave all of their children nice financial gifts. They rented a much nicer home than they could afford to buy and furnished it with top-of-the-line furniture.

She confided in me that she wished they had spent the money more wisely. At the rate they were spending, the money did not last long. Today, her hours have been cut at work. She is the only one in the household working. Her husband became very ill, and he is now on disability. The cars they purchased are now old and broken down. The furniture is also in a state of disrepair. It did not last as long as they had hoped. They had to move to a smaller place. The rent kept going up, and they could no longer afford their nice rented home. Right now, financially, they are just holding on by their fingernails. If they had put a little money aside for the future or made some type of investment for hard times, their struggle now would not be as difficult. The pictures they have of their tour to Europe are all that comforts them. No one can take away their memories.

As I talked to this friend, it became clear to me why, in the beginning, so many challenges were put in front of me. God knew that a lot of difficult situations lay before me. He was making me stronger and wiser so that I could adequately deal with these challenges. The real-estate market went boom and bust three times. It took all my strength to hold on. Every insecurity in my being was tested. I questioned my own positions countless times. When the sun rose over those dark times, things were even better than before the market went down. I had been tested and learned to survive when times were very lean. I was not afraid. The Bible talks about seven years of prosperity followed by seven years of famine. During the prosperity years, you have to store away because the famine will come.

Real estate goes up and down in similar cycles, but the end result is always up. When God made the earth, he only created so much land. There are going to always be more people, but never more land. Get your own piece of the rock. You have just got to be strong enough and wise enough to hold on.

I promised God that if he blessed me with $1 million just once, I would be set for life. He did, and I am. Being faithful over the seed, I was blessed with the harvest. The harvest was ripe.

CHAPTER 4

MY FOREVER HOME

I quickly learned the value of being stable and having your own home. Since I was twenty-two years old, I have been blessed with having my own car and my own house. Being in this position has allowed me to take advantage of many opportunities that would otherwise have been out of reach.

During the seven years that I was in the military, I moved my family quite often because of my job assignments. When I got out of the military, I vowed to put down roots and make a home in which my family and I could grow with each other. I wanted to have a place where we could spend the rest of our lives making good memories.

I talk about how I got my forever home in my first book entitled, *When You Fall Down—Get Up*! If you have not yet read this book, you should pick up a copy at your first opportunity. It really makes this whole real-estate thing come together a lot more clearly.

My sister Jessie helped me buy a house big enough for the kids and me. It had four bedrooms, two baths, and a two-car garage. It was on a corner lot in a nice neighborhood. The bad thing is that it was in terrible condition. Every window was broken and boarded up.

It had been sitting vacant for years, and homeless people had gotten in and used it for a shelter when it was cold outside. To keep themselves warm, they had set fires in the middle of the floor. So even though the house had hardwood floors, there were big circular burn spots in them from the fires. The upstairs bath, sink, and toilet were missing. The bathtub was awful; it was filled a quarter of the way with green fluid when we first saw it.

I almost did not go in to look at it. There was a disgusting smell all through the house. The Realtor who was showing it met everyone on the front porch and explained to them that it was the same house as the one across the street. The only difference is that the one across the street was selling for $150,000, and the one he was showing was only selling for $85,000. It had built-in equity.

He also explained that it was a Housing and Urban Development (HUD) house. It had been winterized, and all the water had been turned off. Someone had used the bathroom in the basement and did the number two. Only after using it was it realized that the toilet had no water to flush. The mess was left there, no one knows for how long. The stench was unbearable. He said if we held our noses, we could see upstairs, but he cautioned us about going into the basement.

Most people got a whiff of the smell and would not go into the house at all. A few ventured upstairs. I looked upstairs and liked what I saw. I could see a hidden jewel. To me, the real value in the house was the space. We needed a four bedroom home. The main level had two bedrooms and a full bath. The other two bedrooms and the bath in the basement meant the kids and I could spread out. We would not be cramped like we were now. All of us could have our own rooms.

I had to see the layout. I had to see if the basement could work for us. I could afford the price. I had a little money to fix things, and I vowed to do everything else myself. I summoned up my courage, held my nose, and ventured into the basement. It had a huge recreation room, a huge bedroom, and a smaller bedroom. The bath was rough, but there was space for a shower and a washer and dryer.

The seat to the toilet was up, and I saw two black, decaying turds in there. Someone had also torn down the curtain, used it to wipe their behind, and just left it laying there. I thought, "Okay, I can clean this up. This is the finest house I have ever seen." I had been holding my breath most of the time and was out of air. Like a mad woman, I made a dash for the upstairs front door. Zooming past the Realtor, I ran to the street and immediately threw up. The Realtor said, "I told you not to go down there!" I thanked him for his time and left.

The wheels in my head started turning. How could I get this house? Because of the settlement on my duplex, I had money for the down payment and closing cost, but my credit was shot. I wanted this house. It was a palace to me. It was my dream home. My sister Jessie helped me get my forever dream home, and I cried. This was so exciting; I had found a new purpose in life: to make ugly houses PRETTY!

I purchased my forever home because I was tired of moving my family from place to place. The type of housing we procured had always been totally dependent on our landlord's mood. The rent on a two-bedroom was all I could afford. I had three children. The landlords with decent housing would not rent a two-bedroom unit to me with me since I had three children. That was too many people for the unit. It just seemed so clear to me. If I was going to pay all the money it took to rent a three-bedroom unit, I might as well buy a home for my family and myself. It made no sense to me to throw that much money out of the window with nothing to show for it.

I purchased my first home for economic reasons. I purchased my forever home because we were ready to put down roots in a stable community. It took all day to move in. I enlisted the help of all my strong nephews, and we used a twenty-four-foot U-Haul truck to transport everything. (We had a lot of pizza and beer to get us through the day.) I vowed never to move again. They would have to take me from this house in a hearse. That was twenty-six years ago.

I have the best neighbors in the world. They are jewels. I would not trade them for anything. Kevin and Lee are also special. Their boys cut my lawn and shovel my snow. As I got up in years and slowed down, these were services that I definitely needed.

I purchased the house twenty-six years ago for $58,000. The last appraisal was $386,000. Over the last twenty-six years, the house has gone up an average of $12,615 per year. That is an increase of over 7 percent a year. Many of my properties did this well. In an economic environment where less than a 1 percent return on your money is standard, this is a phenomenal return. I do not know of any other way to grow your money this fast.

It is like we were paid over $12,615 a year simply to live in and enjoy our home. We lived there for free and were even paid for the convenience. This benefit of home ownership is not available to renters. The rent goes up more and more over the years. The financial burden becomes overwhelming. This forces many families onto the streets. To quote President Barack Obama, "It is not rocket science. It is just math." Home ownership has remarkable benefits. I was even able to pull cash out of the house when I got in a financial strain. (This option is recommended only in emergencies.) As soon as you can, make it happen. Buy your own home. If you can rent, you can buy. Make it happen.

When I retire, I can sell my four-bedroom, two-bath home and get a little one-bedroom

36

efficiency. I can pay cash for the efficiency and still have enough profit from the sale of my house to live comfortably for a couple of decades. This is a good deal. I do not know why everyone does not do this. It just makes so much sense.

Turning our forever home into our dream home was a slow and steady process. We made major renovations almost every year. Our list of improvements to be made was a long one:

- Remodel bath #1
- Replace carpet
- Landscape front yard
- Landscape backyard
- Tuck-point bricks
- Storage shed
- New garage door with opener
- Plant trees
- Patio
- New furnace and air conditioner
- New roof
- Remodel bath #2
- Install patio cover
- Remodel kitchen

- Fireplace gas logs
- Remodel bedroom #1 and #2
- Remodel bedroom #3 and #4
- Replace gutters
- Replace exterior shutters
- Remodel front porch
- New living-room furniture
- New dining-room furniture
- New recreation-room furniture
- New bedroom furniture
- New energy-efficient windows

The renovations typically cost several thousand dollars. You have to believe that you are worth it. It is important to buy things of lasting quality. You want these improvements to outlast you. This is your home: your sanctuary from the storm, your peace from the world, your stable rock for your children, your retirement account, your piggy bank, and your pride and joy. Having your own home is like living rent-free. Every dollar you spend counts for something. The money is not just going into a black hole like it does when you rent. Each dollar benefits you and your family, both now and in the future.

You cannot go overboard and overbuild for your neighborhood. Generally, modest improvements on your home will prove to be excellent investments. When you look back, you will, more often than not, think that your home was the best purchase you ever made.

Owning your own home is not without effort. In order to keep your piece of the rock in top condition, there are some routine maintenance items that must be done on a regular basis. Every year, at a minimum, I would do the following:

- Clean the gutters.
- Service the furnace.
- Service the air conditioner.
- Drain the water heater.
- Aerate the lawn in the spring.
- Aerate the lawn in the fall.
- Fertilize the lawn in the spring.
- Spread weed killer in the spring.
- Power-rake the lawn in spring every other year.
- Winterize lawn in the fall.

My home was sixty years old when I purchased it. If it is properly cared for, I know it will last another sixty years. You also have to get the best homeowners' insurance you can afford. Your home is a big investment. You want to protect it from a catastrophic loss.

As soon as you possibly can, buy your own home. If you are ready to settle down, it will prove to be one of the smartest things you have ever done.

CHAPTER 5

WORKING HARD FOR THE MONEY

I work hard for my money. I am not going to just bundle it up and give it to someone else. I did this before, and it turned out badly for me. My real-estate portfolio was growing in leaps and bounds. Its value was so high that it scared me. I decided I needed to talk to a financial planner. This financial planner told me I was too heavily invested in real estate. I needed to liquidate some of my portfolio and diversify.

My portfolio yielded $250,000 on the partial liquidation. The financial planner suggested I put the money in stocks and bonds. I knew nothing about this area. My expertise was real estate. I gave $250,000 to my financial planner so he could invest the money. He assured me that he was an expert and that my money would grow quickly. In two years, every last penny was gone. My $250,000 stock and bond portfolio went to zero.

That was scary to me. It took fifteen years of blood, sweat, and tears to earn that $250,000, and it was gone in less than two years. That was a valuable lesson for me. Stick with what you know. Find out everything you can about what you do, and learn to do it so well that to quote Reverend Dr. Martin Luther King, "the living, the dead, and the unborn cannot do it better." Knowledge is the key.

Just because some people have fancy titles behind their names does not mean they are more capable than you. Titles do not necessarily mean that people actually know what they are doing. I could have paid myself while I was learning and lost the $250,000 slower than my financial planner. I call this my $250,000 financial education. I get to write this loss off on my income taxes at $3,000 a year until I die.

No one will pay more attention to your money than you.

A piece of real estate is far more valuable than a stock. It can never go to zero. You can touch the bricks, kick the walls, and walk on the lawn. It will always have value.

When I hired the financial planner, I did not want to be bothered with managing my own money. It seemed so much easier to let someone else do it. Learning about stocks and bonds and the stock market seemed like such a hassle. Now I know that you need to understand your own money. You need to understand, for yourself, ways to grow your money that work for you.

Trust, but verify. Your accountant, lawyer, and stock broker do not always have your best interests at heart. Understand what your money is doing. Make sure it is working hard for you. It takes a little time to ask questions and educate yourself, but it is better than sleeping under a bridge on a cold night when all your money is gone.

Having money is just like owning a car. It is a luxury, but if you do things properly, it will make you ten times more than what it costs you every month. Owning a car is very expensive. I remember a sign on the local bus that said, "Save your children $10,000 a year. Buy them a bus pass." It is terrifying to think of how much a car costs to operate.

Monthly Car Expenses	Dollar Amount
Car Payment	$300
Car Insurance	$200
Gas	$150
Maintenance	$150
Registration and License	$50
Total Monthly Expense:	**$850**
Total Yearly Expense:	**$10,200**

This is for an inexpensive car. If you want something fancy, it will easily cost over $15,000 a year. If not used properly, a car can destroy you financially. It can also ruin the rest of your life.

I went to court to fight a speeding ticket that said I was going five miles over the speed limit.

The ticket was $159, and I was upset. Why was the ticket so much?

When I got to court, I was shocked. My ticket did not seem like much anymore. The judge said upfront that the fine for driving with no insurance was $900 and possible jail time. One man was found guilty of driving with no driver's license, no vehicle registration, and no insurance. His friend had sold him the car for $500. The judge gave him a $2,600 fine. If he did not pay the fine, a warrant would be issued for his arrest. If this man had only $500 for a car, how was he going to get the money for a $2,600 fine? He was destined to go to jail. He was in a bad situation.

When the judge called my name, I pleaded guilty and gladly paid my $159 fine. (It ended up being $189 with court costs added.) Feeling blessed that God had opened my eyes; I vowed to keep my heavy foot light on the gas pedal. Maybe I would even take the bus more. An automobile has related expenses so high they are hard to comprehend. For example, the minimum fine for driving under the influence of drugs or alcohol (DUI) is $10,000. You have to add in court costs, penalties, classes, attorney fees, a car alcohol blower, and various other related expenses, you can kiss $10,000 good-bye.

I do property management and have to do a routine credit report before I can rent to a new tenant. One young woman had a $100,000 judgment on her credit report from Allstate Insurance. Never having seen anything quite like that before and thinking it was a mistake, I called and asked her about it.

The young woman told me a story about when she had just bought her first car. She did not have enough money to get auto insurance and was going to get the insurance on her next payday.

Before that pay day, however, she had an accident. One night she was driving and all she remembers is feeling a bump. She saw two legs go up the front windshield and over the top of the car. She was young and inexperienced and realized she has struck a pedestrian that came out of nowhere.

The man she hit was hurt badly and had many medical bills. He sued her, and a $100,000 judgment was put against her. The judgment had haunted her for years. It would not go away. Now she was ready to graduate from school and start a new job with great pay.

I told this young woman I could not rent to her. Even if she got a job making a whole lot of money, there was a $100,000 court judgment against her. It was going to take a long time to pay that off. If she got a job, her check was going to be garnished to pay off the judgment. The court was going to take a great deal of her money. This was not going to leave her enough money to pay the rest of her bills. She would not be able to pay her rent because she would be paying her judgment. I could not afford to take care of her by letting her stay in my place for free.

The woman cried and pleaded with me to give her a chance. She was sure she could figure things out. I had to tell her that I could not do it. This was a bad situation, and I was not going to put myself in the middle of it. She cried so hard, but there was nothing I could do. Her life would be ruined for a long time.

Who has this kind of money? Think really hard about how cool it will feel to be behind the wheel of your own car. It could end up being the worst mistake you could ever make.

On the other hand, having a car presents you with unlimited opportunities for making even more money. You can take a higher-paying job that is not on a bus route and show up every day on time. You can work two jobs that are far apart. Because you have dependable transportation, you can get to both on time.

You don't have to take a cab to buy groceries, go to the Laundromat, or go out on the town. You can drive the whole family to a vacation spot versus having to fly. You also do not have to rent a car once you get to your destination in order to see the local sights.

If your boss needs something done at the drop of a dime, you can jump in your car and get it done before the deadline. This will, many times, earn you a raise for being such a valuable employee. You can haul heavy items in your vehicle that you cannot carry on the bus. This saves you many expensive delivery charges. You can get a cheaper apartment, not on a bus route, and save a ton of money.

I was told I had to take care of my car. If I changed the oil regularly and kept it licensed, registered, insured, and full of gas, it would always get me to where I wanted to go.

That is the way it is with money. You have to gas it up. This means you are getting a return on your investment. You are not just spending every dime you are making. You are putting aside 10 percent of everything you earn and making it work for you. You are making investments in real estate, businesses, stock, bonds, and other enterprises to make sure you always have resources to protect your money and to fill up your tank.

Having money is just like owning a car. If you take care of your money by putting gas in it, keeping the oil changed, and keeping it legal, it will be there for you to do whatever you need it to do. If you spend like there is no tomorrow and get down to your last dime, you will find yourself broke and stranded.

This gets back to the main premise learned in the book *Personal Finance for Dummies*.

- Save 10 percent of everything you earn.
- Spend less than you earn.
- Save what you do not spend.
- Invest what you save.

Have a spending plan. When the allotted money is gone, stop spending. Make sure your money is working harder for you than you had to work to get each and every dollar.

I attended a very interesting financial seminar. I have gone to hundreds of these seminars, and I am always eager and present. If the seminar is giving out free information, I am going to be there. I have even, on a few occasions, paid to get information. (Free is my preference, however.)

If you pick up one idea that helps you in your financial life, it is worth the two to three hours of the time you spent.

At this particular financial seminar, the speaker was talking about what to do when you come into an unexpected windfall of money. It was referred to as the "Rule of 10-10-10-70." It went as follows:

- 10 percent: Save. Put away for you.
- 10 percent: Give it away. Pay to a charity or the disadvantaged.
- 10 percent: Blow on anything you ever thought you wanted.
- 70 percent: Invest in yourself and your future.
  - i. Reliable auto
  - ii. Education
  - iii. Business opportunity
  - iv. Buy a home, etc.
  - v. Retirement savings

The investment medium I used to gas up my money was real estate. I have done very well in this area. Wanting more than one area of expertise, I also tried my hand at stocks and bonds. I did not make a dime. Instead, I lost $250,000. Maybe I should just stick to what I know.

You cannot get your investment house in order unless you have your personal house in order. You need to make sure you always have a cash reserve. You will need this if an emergency presents itself that leaves you short of cash. Believe me, this happens more than you think.

Those who rode out the last real-estate downturn had a big chunk of cash put away for hard times. This is called reserves. When you are a real-estate investor, it is not unusual for the bank to require reserve cash somewhere that equals six months of the payments you have on each of your mortgages. This must be in place before they will give you a loan. You cannot spend everything you get. If the water heater goes out, the roof starts to leak, or the furnace dies, money has to be there to take care of these things. They cannot be ignored.

Always save 10 percent of everything you earn. Make sure you do your income taxes every year and pay whatever is due. Pay your bills, and pay them on time. This will always give you an outstanding credit report. Good credit is worth more than a pot of gold. With good credit you can use a small amount of money to control very large assets. This is called leverage.

Setting goals is so important. Always know where you are going, how you are going to get there, how long it is going to take, and what you are going to do when you get there.

In my adult lifetime, I have been through three real-estate upswings and downturns. We call these booms and busts. You have to have a plan, and you have to work your plan. Decide how you will handle every possible situation that can predictably occur. This way, if the situation occurs, you can react calmly and thoughtfully rather than erratically.

Life is just like real estate; it goes in approximately seven-year cycles. It goes up awhile, and then it goes down. Knowing this information, you can have a plan and make it work. It will feel good when your plan comes together. When times are good, put away for a rainy day. When it rains (and it will), you will be prepared.

You work hard for your money. If you spend eight hours making a dollar, you should spend twelve hours watching that money to make sure it works just as hard for you as you worked for it. If you are young, you will not be able to work as hard as you do now when you are older. Make sure that when you get older, the money you made when you were younger is still there to work for you in your senior years.

If you choose to go into real-estate investing, read three or four books on real-estate investing. Take a real-estate investing course at the local community college. Do not go in cold and blind. Arm yourself with as much information as you possibly can. Learn how the successful have handled different situations. When that great opportunity presents itself, jump in with both feet, and do not look back.

CHAPTER 6

PRAYER

Being a landlord has brought me to my knees many times. Over the last thirty years, there have been good deals and bad deals. A song came over the radio recently that summed up my real-estate investing experience. It was called, "I Found the Answer, I Learned to Pray," by Mahalia Jackson.

I tried managing the high-end rental properties. I could not understand the guy with a trust fund who could not pay his rent because he spent all of his money buying drugs. It was also hard to feel sorry for the woman with a six-figure executive job who could not pay her rent because Nordstrom's Department Store was having a great sale. Rich people and poor people have similar problems, but for different reasons.

The low-income properties were my stomping ground. I was poor all my life. I had a better understanding of the plight of the poor. I understood poor people who were just trying to survive and keep a roof over their heads.

This was the area where I could be the most effective. It came with a lot of hassle, but it also came with a lot of profit potential. The return on investment was more than anything I could have imagined.

During my many times of prayer, the same message came back to me over and over. It became clear to me that this real estate was how I would be blessed. My pool of tenants would include alcoholics, drug addicts, men with no jobs, and women with eight children. I would have to deal with people who had given up or who just needed a little break. These people were the world's forgotten and downtrodden.

Prayer let me know that for every 100 people who spit on me, betrayed me, stole from me, lied to me, moved out in the middle of the night, or borrowed money from me and did not pay me back, one soul would find its way out of the darkness. One soul would be lifted up.

At that point, a good mark would be put in the Good Book in heaven in my name. That is where my true riches and blessings really lie. That is true treasure. Matthew 6:21 says, "Where your treasure is, there will your heart be also."

It is fun to watch the children when you show a rental that you have made really nice. They are so uninhibited. They run from room to room saying, "This is really nice. The carpet is clean, and it already has curtains." They start claiming their rooms, and they talk of the birthday parties they will have in the backyard. It is evident they never had anything quite this nice before. You are happy you can provide them with a positive experience.

You have to teach them how to take care of their new place, how to keep it clean and in good repair. Many times people simply do not know these things. As a landlord you have to require that all your tenants have their own renter's insurance policy. Just in case they miss a payment because funds are tight, make sure you have a backup policy of your own. The tenant still has to pay, but your insurance will go after them for the money, and you won't have to worry about this.

I have so many stories from my time as a real-estate agent, and so many prayers.

Lord, help me to forgive the tenant who called me and told me his son had driven the car through the bedroom window and the car was resting on the bed. His son was just upset and thought he was pushing the brake when he was really pushing the gas. He did not mean it. His father gave me his last $2,000 toward repairs. This left me just a few thousand dollars short after the insurance payment. The repair took months, as there were a lot of surprise expenses. The father and son ended up homeless.

Lord, help me have compassion for the man who said I have no heart. He took his rent money to the gambling casino in an effort to stretch it into enough to also buy groceries. He lost everything.

When he told me the story, he kept saying, "Don't you see? Don't you understand? It's not my fault. Those slot machines took all my money! You should understand that I can't pay you." He was in denial that any of this was his fault.

As the sheriff drove up to evict him, he was sitting in his easy chair watching TV. He watched in disbelief as we took every single thing he owned and put it on the front lawn. We had the locks changed so he had no way to reenter. This man said it was entirely my fault. He said that I should understand that he no longer had any money. He said I had no heart. Lord, help me understand this type of thinking.

Please help me forgive the woman who was smoking in bed and caught the mattress on fire. I thank you for my insurance agent who had previously let me know you need a separate insurance policy on the interior of a condo or townhome. The homeowners' association (HOA) has an insurance policy, but it only covers the exterior of the building and has a very high deductible.

Thank you for letting me listen to him when he said $10,000 would not cover much and that I would need a more comprehensive policy. I thought he was just trying to get more money out of me. He had me purchase the Cadillac Policy. I had every coverage imaginable and needed it all. The most helpful was the "ordinance law regulation" upgrade.

A regular policy puts your property back the way it was when you bought it. It does not cover any building-code updates that may have occurred over the years that you owned it. If the plumbing, heating, electric, or anything else has to be brought up to code, this comes out of your pocket.

These costs can be very expensive. The coverage only kicks in with a loss of over 50 percent of the value of the property, but it can save the homeowner thousands of dollars. You may never need it, but if you do, it is good to have. The cost is worth the peace of mind. The total cost of the fire caused by the smoking tenant was over $60,000. Because if my excellent insurance, I had to come out of pocket with very little of this.

It takes almost a year of your life to put things back together after a significant fire. It takes a lot of time and effort and is something you do not ever want to go through again.

Please help me forgive the young new mom who backed up the sewer line with baby wipes. The box said you could flush these wipes. If she had been feeling better, she would have gone down to the basement to check. Before the smell forced her to investigate, she would have seen that it was filled with two inches of raw sewage. All the water she was running upstairs was backing up into the basement downstairs. We had to call out the toxic-waste team. It was half a year before the house was habitable again.

Thank you for allowing me to witness the young family with four kids work their way off the Section 8 housing program and into the joy of home ownership. The first few years were rough. They struggled every month to pay their part of the rent, but it was paid consistently. The water was turned off a few times, as was the gas and electricity. Still they pressed forward.

The husband went to jail for driving without auto insurance. There was just not enough money to go around. I helped where I could but knew they had to find their own way. Finally, the husband's job turned full time.

They were a praying family, and they stayed positive. I gave them one small loan, and they paid back every cent. This loan helped them make the down payment on their new home. They insisted that I come to their housewarming party. The husband's dad thanked me for making this possible for his kids. They were so proud. Being a landlord is challenging, but it can also be a very rewarding job.

Thank you for the tenant who stayed twelve years. She left the place better than she found it. The grass was plush, green, and weed-free. The carpet was shampooed and still looked new. The bathrooms were spit-shined. The ceramic tile was gleaming and mold-free. The toilets were so clean you could drink from them. All the walls were washed, and not a single window was broken. In the kitchen, the stove and refrigerator had been broken down, every inch cleaned and put back together. Every trace of grease had been carefully scrubbed from the face of the kitchen cabinets, and the finish was still intact. Thank you for letting me experience this tenant. Thank you for my ability to not only give her entire deposit back, but also to triple it. She restored my faith in being a landlord.

As a result of my career in real estate, every last one of my siblings purchased their own homes. Most of my children did also. I felt like a trailblazer lighting a path for all who came after me. I was highlighting the joy of the great American dream—home ownership. Owning your own home is also an incredible wealth builder. It is where dreams are born and memories are made. It is stability and a good foundation.

Being a real-estate investor is a tough job, especially for a woman. All jobs are hard, for that matter. When being a landlord is bad, it is very bad. When it is good, it is really good. It rewards you morally and financially better than anything else you could imagine.

CHAPTER 7

CALIFORNIA

My best real-estate deal of all time was out in California. I found out that my brother-in-law had a condo there that was giving him difficulty. He had gotten it for what seemed like a good price. He told me, "This is California. Everyone knows that California real-estate values go up through the roof." In this situation, that is not exactly what happened.

He bought the property for $124,000. It was a little two-bedroom, two-bath, seven-hundred-square-foot condo. Within one year, he got a job transfer. By then the value had gone down to $119,000. Managing a property yourself, long distance, almost never works. He could not keep a good tenant in the unit. The tenants would be good at first, but then they would stop paying their rent. They quickly realized that there was very little that he could do long distance, so they took advantage of him.

After months, when he finally got a bad tenant out, he had to take off work; fly in; and try to paint, clean, and get the condo ready for the next tenant. He would get it rented, and the nightmare would start all over again. It was costing him thousands and thousands of dollars to pay the mortgage and HOA when it was vacant. He also had to pay to fix any damage done by the previous tenant. To top things off, the value of the condo was going down.

When I talked to him, he was really upset. He said, "I am not putting another dime into that place. The bank can have it back." Understanding his frustration, I asked him to give the property to me. I would give him $2,000, make up the four back payments, and keep all future payments current. This would be much better for his credit. A few months of slow payments would look better on his credit than a foreclosure.

A foreclosure would keep him from buying anything for several years. I told him that I would give him two years to buy the property back from me. If he changed his mind, he had two years to pay me back all the money I had put into the property, plus a small profit. We would tear up the quit-claim deed, and the property would again be his.

He reluctantly agreed, and we had a California lawyer draw up a quit-claim deed and a power of attorney so I could talk to the mortgage company. We did not give the mortgage company the exact details on what we were doing. They sent the mortgage coupons to me, and I kept paying the mortgage.

For four years, the condo had an approximate negative cash flow of $500 a month. The HOA alone was $300. We also had to pay periodic maintenance, and the property manager had to be paid.

We got an extremely good property manager. He was referred by a friend, and the money we paid him was the best money we could have ever spent. During those four years, we only had two tenants, and there were only two months of vacancy. The value, however, dropped to a low point of $99,000. The property manager got as much rent as he could, but the property still had an approximate negative cash flow of $500 a month.

I could not sleep at night. I could not afford the earthquake insurance, and every time I heard on the news that there had been an earthquake in California, my heart stood still. I also found out that if I had died before I sold the condo, we had to set up an estate probate not only in Colorado, where I lived, but also in California, where the property was located. This could be very expensive.

It had been four years, and not only was the condo eating cash, but it was also going down in value. I was beginning to believe I had made a financial mistake. Then, almost overnight, the condo started going up in value by $5,000 a month. In the first year it went up to $150,000. By year two it was up to $200,000.

The condo was going up in value so fast it made me nervous. My property manager called to let me know my tenant was moving in a few months. I had to decide if we were going to look for another tenant for the next year or if I was going to sell the property. I really did not want to put another $500 a month into the property for another year. I also did not know how long this $5,000 a month appreciation could last. The property manager also told me that we would have to find a new property manager, as he was going into full-time investing.

I consulted with lawyers, certified public accountants, Realtors, and my children. We decided to take whatever money we could get and run. We put the condo on the market for $239,000. It was under contract within a few days. In California, you have to set up a property escrow. We closed in about five weeks.

My Realtor got someone to close for me using a power of attorney. He was extremely professional. I had to do very little. All I had to do was to send some money to fix the property up so it would be ready for sale. After that, I only had to wait a short time for the sales proceeds to come by certified mail.

I was able to pay back (to myself) all the money I had put into the property for those four years I fed it; I paid the capital gains taxes and still cleared $100,000 on the deal. It was a very good day for me.

You always wonder if you did the right thing to sell when you did. I continued to monitor the prices on condos in the area. The prices went up well over $400,000 over the next two years. I wanted to kick myself.

Suddenly, just as fast as the prices went up, they started coming down. The California real-estate market went bust. The condo went back down from over $400,000 to $99,000. That is, if you could sell it. Nothing was moving.

If I had held the property through another lease, I would have gotten stuck in the downturn. I may have been unable to sell. Looking back at things, it was a very good decision to sell. In that situation, it had been smart to take the money and run all the way to the bank.

CHAPTER 8

THE SKY IS FALLING!

My sons were now in their twenties and thirties. They both figured I was doing this real-estate thing all wrong. They were going to show me the error of my ways and take my real-estate business to a whole new level. All I could do was hold on for the ride. Heaven help me!

My kids have been helping me with the rental properties since they were in diapers. They always had a cleaning rag in one hand and a paintbrush in the other hand. Now they were very skilled in all aspects of remodeling. They could hang drywall; lay ceramic tile; and do light plumbing, electrical, landscape, and yard maintenance. And no one could beat them at painting. They were very good at what they did. They also added a lot of value to my properties and greatly improved my bottom line.

Once, my son Markus and I went to a real-estate class. He met a woman there who intrigued him. She was older and getting ready to retire. She told him something that stuck with him. This woman had been in real estate for thirty years. She had twelve condos. All of them were paid for, and she had an $8,000 per month positive cash flow. She was going to retire in style. Markus was impressed.

He immediately became a condo expert. Markus was convinced that this was the way to get filthy rich. The HOA does everything for you. You do not have to cut the lawn, fertilize the lawn, shovel the snow, or replace the roof. The housing association did all the exterior maintenance. You did not have to work yourself to death like we had been doing with single-family homes all these years. Like the woman he met at the class, Markus felt you could pay your units off and live on the rental income.

Markus ran this idea by his brother Michael, and they both agreed that condos were the way to go. Both of them put a lot of pressure on me to listen to them and value their opinions. Even though they were young, they had figured a lot of things out. I needed to trust them more and let them have a say in some of my financial matters. I had, after all, always told them that I was building a financial real-estate empire for my kids and grandkids.

I did ask them a few questions:

- What do you have to lose if you are wrong?
- Can you work an extra job and pay me back any money I lose, or will you just say, "I'm sorry; I did not know"?
- What research and expertise went into your opinion?
- Was this opinion a fad or a gut decision?
- Is your gut seasoned? Your gut does not get good at decision making until it has been punched a few times.
- What can you do to help me if listening to you brings me down?

These were things I needed to know. I had listened to them many times before. Both young men had made some excellent judgment calls. I knew that this could be a critical point in their future decision-making ability. I listened and weighed the evidence. In the end the final decision had to be mine. I was the one with all the money on the line. Michael and Markus needed to respect that. After much thought, I decided to buy my first condo.

I had always been taught to buy good, well-situated single-family houses. The tenants stay longer, they take better care of the property, and these houses appreciate in value better. This information had helped me make some profitable decisions. This condo thing now had me thinking pretty hard.

Our first condo had two bedrooms, two baths, and one thousand square feet. The purchase price was $90,000, and I had to put down 20 percent. It was easy to rent, in good condition, and seemed to be low maintenance. In two years it was worth $105,000. I was happy and could get used to this. No yard work. No snow shoveling. I just collected the rent, paid the HOA and mortgage, and pocketed the difference.

This was working so well that I purchased another condo. This time it was a fixer-upper. My son Michael and I were going to be partners. I was to supply the material, and Michael was to supply the labor. We would totally remodel the condo, sell, and split the profit. We would split the profit sixty-forty in my favor. This could be a good inside look for my son on the actual nuts and bolts of how fix and flip transactions were done.

Both Michael and I were excited. We bought for $80,000, were going to put $12,000 into the renovation, and planned to sell for $106,000. In a matter of months, we would split a $14,000 profit.

We ran into problems, however. Materials were a lot more expensive that we realized, and we still had the mortgage payment, HOA, and utility bill to be paid every month while we were fixing the condo. Michael was also a perfectionist.

If he did not like something, he would tear it out and do it all over again. Everything had to be just right.

We were running over budget and behind schedule. To complicate matters more, Michael's job sent him on an out-of-state assignment for several months. He had been working on the condo nights and weekends, and now he could not work on it at all because he was out of town. The mortgage, HOA and utility bills still had to be paid. We had not planned for this.

Michael's out-of-state assignment was extended. The condo was just sitting—unfinished and bleeding money. It was now year two of a project that was supposed to take only a few months. The market turned, and values went down. The condo we were going to make all new and sell for $106,000 was now only worth $28,000. It was a nightmare.

Michael and I talked. We had a hopeful $106,000 nonperforming asset that was half finished. It was now only worth $28,000 and was costing us money every month. We were stuck. If we wanted to maintain our credit, we could not just walk away. We had to pay someone else to finish the condo and rent it out to cover most of our expenses. In twenty years the value might come back.

In the end the condo cost $25,000 to fix instead of the $12,000 we projected. We also had $18,000 in holding costs. To top things off, we paid $80,000, and it was now only worth $28,000. In two years, we saw $95,000 go up in smoke.

Costs	Dollar Amount
Purchase Price	$80,000
Renovation Costs	$25,000
Holding Costs	$18,000
Total Costs:	**$123,000**
Current Value of House:	$28,000
Total Loss (*Total Costs – Current Value*):	**$95,000**

This was an expensive but very valuable lesson for both of us. The condo was not in an especially nice area. The quality of the complex is important. We also over improved the condo we bought in comparison to the other condos in the complex. It looks nice, but you never get your money back this way.

We also learned that condos don't provide cash flow as well as single-family homes because of the extra expense of the HOA. The HOA also goes up every year. It can eventually get higher than your mortgage payment. The HOA has a lot of power even though you are the one paying the mortgage. You also pay the HOA for as long as you own the condo.

You pay a premium for the HOA to cut the grass and shovel the snow. Unlike the situation with a single-family residence, you have no control over these expenses. The HOA also does not pay for all exterior repairs. If you need a new roof, the HOA does a special assessment and asks each owner for extra money to cover the expense. You have no control over anything.

Condos also do not appreciate as well as single-family residences. You are constantly dealing with a great number of different personalities that need to get along. When this does not happen, this can be cause for much grief and expense. The tenant upstairs could be playing his music too loud or his children could be walking too hard on the floor. The tenant in D-122 could be having too many strange people over. The guy next door could be visiting your wife while you are at work or parking in your parking space. The situations you deal with are endless.

I tried condos at the urging of my sons. This avenue did not work for me. Over a period of four years, I lost over $160,000 on two units. You cannot do this every day and come out unhurt.

I again decided to stick to what I know—single-family houses, duplexes, and triplexes (nothing bigger than a fourplex). These types of investments have served me well over the years. Condos were a big adventure—or should I say a big nightmare? I did not like it. Good, solid single-family houses are the way to go for me.

CHAPTER 9

GOLDEN EGGS

I purchased approximately one property every two years. Between 2005 and 2010, I did five deals, and I lost money on all those deals. Had I lost my touch? I had definitely made a tactical error not selling in 2005 when all my associates sold. It was the top of the market at that time. I got greedy, wishing the market would go even higher. Instead the market went straight down. In less than two years, fifteen years of gains were wiped out.

How could this be? I told myself. This is a fluke; the market has to go back up. It has gone up over the last ten years. I kept buying and kept hoping. It was all in vain. The market went even lower. By 2011, my million-dollar portfolio was only worth $400,000.

This was devastating to me. It appeared as if everything I had worked for in the last thirty years was going, going, gone. What was I going to do? I went to real-estate seminars looking for an answer. In one investment seminar, the speaker said you have to know the value of what you have. He said to compare your investments as you have them now to where they would be if you invested them elsewhere.

If I sold everything, I would walk away with $300,000 after sales expenses. If I put this money in a safe money-market account, bond, or certificate of deposit, I would earn $3,000 a year at 1 percent. This would provide me with just $250 a month in steady income for the rest of my life.

I was nearing retirement age. My real estate was supposed to provide me with a comfortable retirement. It would be hard to even feed myself on $250 month. Plus, I would have to pay for housing, utilities, transportation, medical insurance, and other incidentals.

My rental income was higher than $250 a month. If I held on to the properties, in a good month, I would clear nearly ten times that amount ($2,500) after expenses. On a bad month, I would clear $100. If I am optimistic and believe I can consistently clear the higher amount, it turns out to be a lot of money in a year. It is not a great deal of money, but when taken into account that the average person retires on less than $800 a month, it is not so bad. It is a whole lot better than the $250 a month I would retire on if I sold everything right away.

Loving math as I do, I calculated how much money I would need to have sitting in the bank drawing 1 percent interest to produce a yearly income of $25,000. This is the amount I could get on the money when the rental income was at its peak. The results were shocking. My assets were worth over $1 million. The real value was over $3 million. It all depended on how you looked at things.

The value was not in selling the assets and seeing how much cash I could get in hand right away. The real value of the assets was the income stream it produced. This income stream could possibly continue not only for the rest of my lifetime, but also provide a comfortable living for the lifetimes of my children and grandchildren.

Another positive aspect of this income is that it was not stagnant. I could raise the rent periodically as the cost of living increased. I would also still have control of the property and any appreciation that occurred. My tenants would be paying my principal loan balance. At some point, the property would be free and clear with no loan balance. At this point, my cash flow would skyrocket.

This information made me very happy. My life's work had not been in vain. I was sitting on a gold mine and did not even realize it. Sometimes money you get quick, fast and in a hurry is not all it appears to be. Money that comes in slow, steady, and over a prolonged period of time is the real secret to the fountain of wealth.

I was at the library with my grandbaby. The "Jack in the Beanstalk" story caught my interest. I sat down to read it. Jack ended up with the goose that laid the golden eggs. This goose took very good care of Jack and his mother for the remainder of their lives. They shared their good fortune with the whole village.

When both Jack and his mother died, a couple purchased the goose from their estate. They were happy to get the golden eggs at first. Then they wanted more and more of what each golden egg could buy. Instead of being thankful for what they had, they got upset that the goose could only lay one egg a day.

In the end, they needed the golden egg so badly that they killed the goose and cut the golden egg out of her. It is true that they got that golden egg, but they had killed the goose that laid it. They never got another golden egg. Soon they lost everything they had. *Quick money is not always good money!*

I met two men. They were both fifty-six years old. I will call the first man DEH. He was living on a small disability pension. He was on Section 8 low-income housing, had done two short stints in prison, had several children that he could not afford to care for, and was just getting by. He was smart and hardworking and could do anything you asked him to do. He said his grandmother raised him. They did not have much, so he had to figure out how to make do with what they had. He had a lot of ingenuity.

This man got me through the darkest period in the real-estate downturn. He prayed for me, encouraged me, fixed anything I had that was broken, and encouraged me not to give up at a time when I had lost all hope. I no longer wanted to be a landlord, stressing out over these rental properties. This man told me he wished he had rental properties to be stressed out over. It was clear to him that God had blessed me with these rental properties for a reason. He knew I would use them to help as many people as I could.

His talent was his knowledge of the Bible, his ability to fix anything, and his ability to realize that even though he did not have as much as some people, he was still blessed. He had a little money coming in, a little place to live in that had heat and lights, and food in the refrigerator. It was not as much as some people had, but it was still a blessing. There were some people doing so much better, but there were other people doing a whole lot worse. God used all kinds of threads to create the beautiful tapestry called life. No thread was more important than another. All the threads—long and short, fat and skinny, colorful and dull—were needed. I knew this man was right, and I felt so ungrateful. There was a reason why I was a landlord.

I will call the second man Isaiah. When I met him, he was getting ready to retire in a few years. He had been on his job over thirty years and had his own house, several cars, and a six-figure savings account. He had even bought a home for his mom. He was intelligent and hardworking, and he had clearly figured life out.

The fortune these two men had met in life was like night and day. Isaiah told me this:

> Life is all about choices. You can have anything you want in life. You must first want

it bad enough, know you can get it, and do everything you can to make it happen.

You may have had the best of training, advice, and upbringing life can provide, but in the end the outcome is up to you. You have to take steps and make the decisions to bring your own dreams into your own life. No one can do it for you. You have to make it happen for yourself.

You have to take responsibility for your own life. You have to look far into the future. Think about everything before you do it. You hope for the best, but think if you could live with the worst thing that could happen? If you can't, then that might not be the best thing to do.

It is not the short dollar or the quick dollar that counts, but the long dollar or future dollar that matters. You have to be concerned with what this will do for you in the future.

I asked myself many times, how did things turn out so well for me? God had me; the whole time he had me in the palm of his mighty hand. He is given all the glory and was ordering my steps, even in my worst times. I suffer from depression. I will always fight an invisible demon. But that demon will never win. As long as I keep fighting, I have a chance. If I quit, the only thing that is certain is that I will lose the game.

The first man I met is also still fighting. He has gone back to the things that his grandmother and God taught him. It is like he has been wandering through the wilderness for a long time. I know that even at fifty-six years old, he can find his promised land. God has goodness and blessings stored up for him too bountiful for him to comprehend. Both of these men have been like angels in my life.

Even in this depressed economy, I am still a millionaire. But getting there was so hard. It took over thirty years. I worked many long hours over the years, laying my foundation. I worked hard but loved my job so much. It did not feel like work at all. I loved what I was doing. I was doing it for my family, so I just did what had to be done. I was not paid a dime.

You do something long enough, and you become an expert by default. You have seen every problem, and you know how to fix it. Like I said previously "no one living, dead, or unborn can do it better than you." This was something Reverend Dr. Martin Luther King Jr. quoted often. Find what it is you love to do in life, and become the very best at it. It is not going to be an easy fight, but the prize is worth the battle.

My real estate is like the goose that laid the golden eggs. As long as I hold on to it and take care of it, I will get a golden egg at the end of every month. Real estate, to me, has more value than paper stocks or bonds. Its value will never go to zero. I can walk on the grass of the lawn, kick the bricks, and know what I have is real. A house can provide my family and myself shelter when all else fails.

I see what I need to do. I will hold on to my real estate with everything I have inside of me. Its value is infinite. I have no intention of killing the goose that lays me golden eggs.

CHAPTER 10

THE LAST BOOM

I sit in a lounge chair on the beach on some tropical island off the Gulf of Mexico. Last night I danced the night away. Tonight I sip on a piña colada. The waves go out and come in with big white billows. I hear the crashing sound they make as they meet the still water already on the shore.

The wind gently caresses my face, and the sun softly warms my skin. I hear the seagulls in the background. The sky is a brilliant blue, dotted with big, white, fluffy clouds.

This is so beautiful; so peaceful. Why did I not even know something like this existed? I did not even want to come with my sister. Fifteen hundred dollars was much too much money to spend on a trip for myself. She also has a stressful job and has learned over the years how to recharge her batteries. This was something I still needed to learn.

I have been a real-estate investor for over thirty years. My days are filled with phone calls: "The toilet is stopped up; the water heater flooded the basement; the kitchen is on fire; I don't have the rent; bedbugs are biting me; the car went through the garage door; the dog bit the neighbor; the people next door are making too much noise."

You meet the plumber, the carpenter, the electrician, and the appliance guy and you make three trips to the bank. The mortgages have to be paid, as do all the repair, gas, electric, and water bills. The lawn guy calls. He has not yet been paid. It is the end of the month. You could have sworn everyone was paid. This month, there is supposed to be $2,500 left in the bank account. It is just not there.

You make another trip to the bank. You wrote two large checks for repairs that you neglected to put in the check register. The lawn guy has to wait until next month. He threatens to stop cutting the lawns. You have the nicest lawns on the block. You go into your personal funds to get him paid. For the millionth time, you ask yourself, "Why am I paying to do this job?"

The next month, the circus starts all over again. You cannot go on vacation when this is your life. If your tenants cannot contact you for even one day, they lose their minds and do things you would not believe. All you can wonder is, "What were they thinking?" You know this is going to be an expensive mess to fix.

I have done well in real estate. At what point will I be satisfied? At what point will I have enough? I wanted to leave my children set for life. They would not have to worry about anything. Maybe they should have to worry a little. Maybe I should rethink this real-estate thing.

Reality sets in. I am sixty years old and tired. The pace that keeps me going from sunup till sundown is no longer sustainable. I am now old and sick. It is time to harvest some of the fruits of my labor.

I have purchased at least one rental property every two years for the last thirty years. I sold almost nothing. My portfolio is too big and too unmanageable. There is now more than I can handle. The only way I was able to take a vacation was because I hired a property manager to help me temporarily.

The market is now red hot. In the last three years, some properties have doubled from their low. For the seven previous years, the real-estate market—and all the financial markets, for that matter—lost as much as 50 percent of their value. The market went down so quickly and stayed down for so long that it felt like the economy would never recover.

A young black president named Barack Hussein Obama was nominated to the highest office in the United States. He really turned things around. Unemployment went from 11 percent to 5 percent. The budget deficit was cut in half.

The stock market Dow went from 6700 to 17800. This is an all-time high, and most real-estate markets across the country are in full recovery mode. The Denver real-estate market is doing especially well.

It is well known that the real-estate market goes in high and low cycles. Over my thirty years in the business, I have gone through several booms and busts. We are in the middle of a boom. The market will not stay up forever. I asked myself, am I strong and brave enough to ride out another real-estate cycle? During the last downturn, I prayed. I told God that if he let me get any of my million dollars back, I would take my money off the table. He did, and I am sticking to my word. It is time to sell.

The long-term real-estate hold is a rich man's game. Sometimes you need cash infusions to hold things together. People say that you can buy real estate with no money. That has not been my experience. The mortgage payments have to be paid whether the unit is occupied or not. Taxes and insurance have to be paid. Repairs have to be done. Heaven help you if you have no money and the water heater explodes or the roof starts leaking. At some point, you just run out of money and have to sell something to get cash.

I reached a compromise in my life. I decided to sell half my properties and keep the other half. I would use the profit from the properties I sold to pay off the ones I kept. The portfolio was much more manageable this way. I also had available cash to take care of emergencies.

The majority of my money is still tied up in real estate. It will take months or even years to access. This is good for me. If I can get to the money, I will spend it very quickly. That is not a good thing.

I realized that the positive cash flow from the properties I retained was powerful. It was much higher than any interest rate I would get by putting the money in the bank. Most savings accounts are now paying less than 1 percent interest. Cost-of-living increases were built into my cash flow, as

I could periodically raise the rent. The property was also appreciating in value.

I had always been my own property manager before. Permanently keeping the property manager whom I had hired to help me out now seemed so appealing. I _had_ to manage my own properties in the beginning. There was no cash flow, and I was hanging on by my fingernails. You generally have to feed (put money into) a property you acquire for several years before it starts to pay off. The properties I have had for a long time are doing much better. Now I can relax a little.

My property manager manages the tenants, collects the rent, and coordinates the repairs. She is actually more financially efficient than I was. I do not know how she gets things done for much less than I could. I get a check every month, and I only have to worry about how to spend it. This is a win-win situation for me. My property manager gets paid a small percentage, and I get paid the rest, with no brain damage. She is also the most capable property manager I have encountered in a while.

I am getting rid of some of my golden geese. I know these are the problem geese that give me the most headaches. They are old and need much more maintenance, repair, and upkeep than I can manage. Let someone young and energetic have these properties. They will still make money for someone. They just took so much of my time.

This works out well for me. All the struggle, pain, and hard work put in for the last thirty years got me to this point. I have a perpetual income stream that will sustain me through a nice retirement. Maybe after I die, there will still be some money left over for my children. I have taught them well. They have to find their own way.

For right now, I want to bury my toes in more sand at the beach, feel the waves crashing in around my calves, and watch a magnificent orange, red, purple, and blue sunset, while I sip the piña colada in my hand. Life is so good!

AUTHOR BIOGRAPHY

Ella M. Coney has been a real-estate investor in Denver, Colorado, for over thirty years.

She was bitten by the real-estate bug during the real-estate market crash of the mid-eighties. A good friend mentored her through this journey. She took a real-estate investing class at what was then Metropolitan State College of Denver, Colorado. With the help of this class and her mentor, she jumped in with both feet. Real estate was cheaper than it had been in a long time.

Ms. Coney has a Bachelor of Science degree in computer and management science. After determining that this career choice did not suit her, she went back to school and got a Bachelor of Science degree in finance, with a real-estate emphasis. Both of these degrees were from the now new and improved Metropolitan State University of Denver. It has been "transforming lives for over fifty years."

She is now a retired real-estate property manager and investor. Her new job will be, to quote her son's words, "to roam the country in search of adventure."

54025521R00065

Made in the USA
San Bernardino, CA
05 October 2017